solstice

solstice

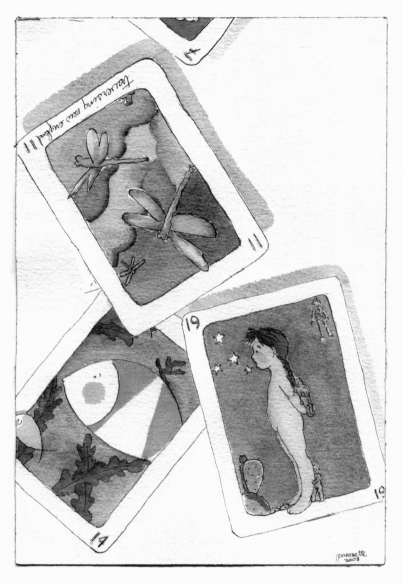

emmy pérez

ISBN: 1-930454-21-X

Swan Scythe Press
2052 Calaveras Avenue
Davis, CA 95616-3021
www.swanscythe.com

Editor: Sandra McPherson
Associate Editor: Maria Melendez
Editor-at-Large: Francisco Aragón
Illustrations and Cover Art: Joan Parazette
Book Design: Eric Gudas
Cover Design: Mark Deamer

CONTENTS

"The door has no door, yet I can go into my outside and love both what I see and what I do not see."

—*Mahmoud Darwish*

for Antonio, Indio Del Sol

SOLSTICE

the americas

War in sun country
Lights water with orphans.

Braids sawed off. As if arms.

Pray for snow, and thistle
Blooms purple along

Roads. Amaranth grows
Beyond the harvest.

*

Morning sky: more meadow
Than metal. A clear-eyed orphan

With stars on her tongue,

Hiding her siblings
In the sun glow.

A soldier knows a kiss
Won't open that mouth.

IRRIGATION

I.
In empty acequia
her body
ripped easily:
a husk
shucked in wind.
Her arms, her legs,
bent like tassel silks.

II.
Winter floods
into cotton fields.
The whole town
thigh-deep
in the irrigation ditch,
stabbing catfish
with large pitchforks.
And still, she insists
on the machete,
firm in her hand,
chopping pears
from the cactus
thinking: *this*
is the sweetest red.

III.
She will grow bones
the way a shark
grows teeth.

MADE OF THE SAME

(song of the migrant farm worker)

I.
All things living made of the same.
The black lip of dog, rose petals,
our aureolas, our cocks.

2.
Grapes fill with spray, dropped
from planes zooming across the sky.
Flies fall in heaps, our feet bend to the vines.

3.
In America, the melons are bred
to bear no seeds. At night,
we crawl into their scars and sleep.

FOR LOS MUERTOS

They last longer than eyes, these fossil skulls.
Perpetual smiles make them docile skulls.

Who carved our faces—cheeks, chins, and foreheads?
Bring bread and dulces; we're all huesos and skulls.

So many bones in each of our fingers.
Our knees bend with hinges. Give besos to skulls.

Skull mask on top of mask covering our souls.
Play guitars with no strings like hostile skulls.

Put on a hat and hide your scarred head.
Crosses etched in temples, colossal skulls.

Follow a path of marigold petals.
All depressions are nostrils, calaveras.

Pérez, the name of many old orphans.
Dragonflies linger, sing Nahuatl for skulls.

The Border

Abuelita, old and shaking,
fumbles through her purse
searching for her green card.
There are eight cars ahead
of us—she begins to sweat.

Chiclets, serapes, ceramic piggy banks.
We buy none of these things the gringos do,
only mangos on sticks, roasted white corn
smeared with butter and salt,
tamales steaming from the pot.

Dogs foam at the mouth,
their skins tight on bones,
the street hot on their padded paws.

Last year, the booth stopped us,
searching the camper
with discotec spotlights.

Any animals? Any fruit?

Rigoberto made it over many years ago
in the trunk of a Honda, holding
his breath beneath wool blankets.

I am aware of my East L.A. accent,
father's broken English, the parrot
suffocating in mother's purse.

Any animals? Any fruit?

American citizen.

As we speed off into San Diego,
J.T. and I sigh, and remove
los cuetes, the illegal firecrackers
stuffed safely in our underwear.

HALLIDAY STREET

The men notice the slight swelling
of her chest. The street breathes:
a mirage of gasoline
flooding ghosts of orange groves.
To be a man is to detect
bodies as they soften.

She checks her reflection
in the chrome of his car. Holds still
while strangers scout a path
halfway to her sky. It is good
to have much cake on your behind.
They want to drop silverware; bring food to lips.

Mouths and hands join together; she ought to

say a prayer to Our Lady of Guadalupe.
Light candles for her bowed head.
Use cushions for knees. Kneel. Stained
glass keeps the sun out. A hymn flutters
through exhaust pipes. Outside, wildflowers
bloom through cracks of stone. Worms appear
in puddles of last night's rain.

. . . She smiles for mother as tortas bake into boats.
They will slit them, fill them with meat.
Plums ferment near the ocotillo fence.
Under skins, flesh hums—capillary, sweet.

La Bufadora

Grandmother, in Ensenada
you fall in the street, bloody
your knee like a schoolgirl's.

No es nada—it's nothing
you say, walnut cheeks dry,
palms scraped, bones intact.
The wound between your legs
healed in time. You have
released all your seeds.
Your blood flowing through
my veins, drips puddles to my feet.

Whales blow water
through holes in their heads.
Breathe, Abuelita, breathe.

The Breathing

The sunflower seed cracking in the parrot's beak; the cassava connected to earth, filtering rain; the pink afterbirth of sky, leaf, and beast; the waking from dreams to our loved one's sleeping; the waking from horror to the bells of the distant cathedral; the reverberations of family, gunshots and home traveling in our blood, congealing in the heart, in the stomach; the small strokes weakening brains, erasing equations, retaining: deer drawn on the damp walls of its caves, beats on thick skins of drums, flutes carved from trees, reeds intimate with tongues.

"DEOLA THINKING"—FIRST WINTER

after Cesare Pavese

The snow is what she did not anticipate,
the clean drifts blackening in the exhaust

of her art (a one-dollar store
offering cheap acts in quantity).

Deola is a napkin ring, a rubber band, a hairpin
fracture, a row of prayer

candles sheathed in stickers of saints,
and all her mornings are the morning

after. She sits on her bed, thinking:
If god were a man, would he want me?

10

SOFT-GELLED CAPSULE

My instinct is to flip
off unmarked cabbies.
Two months
away from home,
I'm not conditioned to polite
honking, men looking
only for business.
Underwear advertisements
plastered on buses
are not for those who ride them.
The quick-footed take the subway.
Walking the street feels like the soft
spot in the newborn's head.
I ride the bus to wrap up in a blanket
of paella, near cords I might tug.
I need more abuelitas
dropping quarters and rosary beads.
You can't hear the whimper
of lung and curb
watching the incubator
through a wall of glass.
The roasted chickens hanging
in storefront windows
leave their heads in the soup.
No one can protect the child
harnessed to the father's back.
She is the eye behind his head.

TRAVERSING NEW ENGLAND

The hunter's prize: an adorned deer
bound to a ski rack. Another young
buck scrapes the open tailgate of a truck.
It is the first time the antlers
are only a burden to the body.

Antonio, Indio Del Sol,
bleeding from the gun wound.
Hands that never meet him,
enter him with instruments.
It is too late to save, in a West
Coast hospital, a boy killed for kill.

Dragonflies disappear among carnivorous
plants in the misty bog.
Cranberries are a bloody harvest.
A 7,000 year old Indian
flowers from his sheath of peat.

THE ROOM

She is afraid to die today because her room is disheveled. They will open her, re-create her life on a chart. Scars on her arm from outdated immunizations; the size of her brain; the last meal she ate; the color of ink in her irises; the flesh of her last lover underneath her fingernails; the traces of all past lovers in the vessel of her body, the ravines transporting all their fluids, flowing Pacific or Atlantic according to the Continental Divide; the diseases her organs suffered; the quality of her blood pumped from the kettle of her heart; everything unnecessary scooped out: eggs, liver, lungs, heart. Is afraid of leaving today because her room is disheveled: photos, letters, numerous lovers, medicine, journal entries. Cannot leave today. Looks both ways before crossing the street and returns inside to the evidence.

STRAY ANIMALS

They've cut into your belly
to pull out the poison.
I've come to take you home.
Under white lights and sheets,
you were the stray deer
in the cornfield with manzanilla
eyes. I will never leave you again.
It is your turn to hold on
to my purse strap, through the crowd
of fruit vendors to the bus stop.
Come, I have made a doll for you.
Brown face, black braids, her legs
stitched with the hair the llamas left.
The gypsies parked their wagons
out front. They shake gourds and maracas
to accompany the drumsong of your heart.
Your grandchildren sit on the hills
spooning goat milk candy.
While you were away, the neighbors'
chinchilla factory burned down.
They must now learn how to shear
wool. Come, the lovebird sings.
Your skin weds as we speak.

CASTROVILLE, CALIFORNIA

The church beside the tired
panaderia is empty. All
are smiling at the Artichoke Festival.

Boys with shaved heads
remind me of you and all boys
with brown skin who died young.

They crowd around a roving magician. One hoax
at the expense of their friend, the hesitant volunteer.
Distrust is a child facing the unhappy
stranger who marks coins and Jokers.

The erotic mountain
and silver smoke I can see through
the sad telescope.

You smile with a mouth
full of bones.

Our mothers are sisters.
Their cracked childhood
adobe, my obsession
for dirt. It calls to us from
the Chihuahuan desert,
plaster peeling, attempting to unleash

an inflorescent heart. Farm workers
crouch in lush strawberry fields
with bandannas veiling their mouths.

One harvest a party,
another a swarm.

Fractured stars gather on night
sky. Chipped glyphs, black
tourmaline eyes. Genesis

is exhausting. Tonight
lips are migratory
with kisses, soft as whales
swimming past hay bales. A blue
America. Not a flag, but two continents
surfacing for air.

After Revolution

Sunlight on my eyes, the dead
among my feet. The sacks
of beans, the pumpkins piled in the shed.
                    Even the mice

speak of keeping in this time
of grief. A ditch like a dried-up
lake. Cobs bleaching, teeth.
                    And the shoveling.

Will I recognize you
—me—within the strata
of this new gathering?
                    In the streets,

fireworks kiss hello
a burning sky. Sparks
find their way back
                    into silver.

I catch my reflection in an open-
air market. The flaking skulls
of coconuts have two dulled eyes,
                    milk that may never flow.

THE DRAWER

The drawer carries almost everything she's looking for. Band-aids, safety pins, rubber bands, earring backs, magnets, paper clips, batteries, luggage tags, nail clippers, sugar packets, movie stubs, toothpicks, poker chips, nail polish, cotton swabs, red hot pepper flakes, broken watches, swirled pink and white mints, scratched lenses, lozenges, honey packets, crackers, lipstick, phone numbers, heavy pesos, watercolors, turquoise beads, candlewicks, paper straws, avocado stones, bra straps, incense punks, pumpkin seeds, drink umbrellas, wishbones, dried apricots, lava rocks, cave wind, a bat's shriek, damp smell, subway heat, manhole steam, freeway traffic, a chola's stare, black eyeliner, a vato's gaze, a goatee comb, a parrot's feather, a strap of leather, purse pennies, sand dollars, Pacific ocean sizzling on the shoreline, bubblegum riddles, lip gloss, paleta stick splinters, cherry red firecrackers, postcards written in cap letters—Germany, L.A., Minnesota, Arizona—matchsticks, used envelopes with return addresses, burning stars, earth smell of La Virgen's robe, Diego Rivera's Aztec marketplace—a woman lifting her cotton dress, revealing her bad-ass tatuajes—scarlet New England leaves crumbling at the touch, marbles clanking in a dirty suede pouch, expired film gone through x-ray radiation, lost red blood cells hoarding oxygen, a grand piano headache, pounding pedals, blurred vision, no rosebuds flung on stage, no blank paper for a note, only a scissor, dozens of dried-up pens and plastic pencils without lead but with erasers.

The drawer manufactures during closed for business hours, replenishing the fractures of what she needs.

PIECES OF STARS

Eggs make the world go round. A lady shrimp guards her eggs in a cave. Lobster coral, sturgeon caviar. Blue shells to match the sky in a nest that blends in tree bark. Baby snake eruptions and shiny purple fruit. The egg cracked into the cake mix always has a streak of blood in it. The albumen of snow where the Emperor sits, waiting for his legacy to hatch. The egg is a magnet, calling his instinct to come make it whole. The Big Bang of the universe: radiation blazing, hatching light; particles collide and annihilate; creating galaxies, planets, more volcanoes and ash, more pieces of stars in her belly; igniting blood flow, calling his rain, calling his reign.

SELF-PORTRAIT, WITH FRIDA

How can I ask a wet nurse
to squeeze black smoke from her body

so I can keep mine
inside me, spiraling underwater

like a swirl of dark ink
in your aquarium

filled with halved papayas
and soaked squash flowers

aside a bundle of bananas
with dusky talons?

Thumbprints of red
prickly pear on a white plate—

what kind of terrible
accident would it take

to make me love the sight
of blood? In my garden,

hummingbirds, our warriors
hover in flower-and-song

come back to life
nuzzling sweet nectar

and why do I only hope for butterflies
fluttering near my braid

and a monkey with a chongo
just like me, a gold ribbon

wrapped loosely around our necks?
Frida, I want

to want
as you do

but I am your *bride*
frightened at seeing life opened.

SPILLAGE

Cloth cups with contoured wires hold her milk. Cloth holds her up, preventing spillage.

Why don't we use our hands and knees to get around? Closer to the greenest shoots of grass and let her milk fall as it pleases?

This gravity propelling us toward the sky. She is a line guided up like a tree, perpendicular to the earth. It is her belly, her breasts that insist on being parallel.

He becomes parallel when he sees her parallels.

WITHOUT WHITEWASH

There is no worse sentence
than one of hunger and despair.

So instead I will construct a line
of inquiry where socks hang to dry

like pairs of question marks on the brown
horizon of boys' backs as they bend

in rows of cotton fields. Where is the dirt
road that leads to the bones of centuries-

old adobes, still standing, exposed, without
whitewash, where kids jump in a canal

whose cattails wave shade over an earthen
home like a hand kissing an abuelita's

smile? It is her own fingers that hide
and prize what few pleasures are left

when the footage flashes a good silver
picture behind eyes washed blue

with age. The feeding tube inserted in
her belly button a tendril like a melon's

connected to the soil. Grandmother, what are you
remembering when you cry out *diosito?*

I Am Looking

for you in the bars of Zaragoza,
among mesquite-strewn sand hills, in amaranth

growing wild in cotton
fields. I am looking in government

documents—no one has your picture,
no one remembers your name.

I stand on your bones
in Mt. Carmel cemetery

and even the dusty silk
flowers are missing

from your grave. *Recuerdos
de sus hijos,* your headstone reads

but I am looking for you
in dirt floor adobes and huecos

gathering rain. You are like a jackrabbit
in high grass waiting until

I am almost upon it
before bounding away,

all ears and legs and feet.
With what degree of ultra-

violet shall I ask the bee
to see you in the trumpet

and blanket flowers? Abuelito,
I wonder if someone will

praise my own father
for growing up in a shack

full of relatives and not really knowing
any of them. No one has a picture

to put a face to your name, so my mother
says: *Look at me. Look in the mirror.*

And still I want to ask:
What tells the juniper

to berry pewter-blue?
What tells the cactus pad

to break into ruby nubble
and yellow flower? What tells me

you are jimsonweed blooming
noxious, beautiful on a sand dune?

Upon Seeing Pecan Trees in the Outskirts of El Paso

Rows of living soldiers
stand wounded with winter
until spring returns. Canal
water floods the orchards
and dust storms tear
new leaves. My will to find
you floods this land
of adobe missions
roaming the gypsy
Rio Grande. U.S. citizen

by natural disaster,
are you deerskin
or dirt brick, agave
or scorpion? You wandered
over the bridge and back,
bridge and back for booze
and women, until your family
grew tired and left on a wind-
blown day—sky-brown
eyes crying from the bus window.

Grandfather, I've lived
everywhere, indigenous
to nowhere. Is it possible
to blossom standing still?
Because there is an orchard
of stars in my belly,
reflecting the slow leak
of lake into the desert.

YSLETA, TEXAS

Cottonwood crosses
planted in sun-
cracked mud: Inca dove
bones among olla shards.
In this desert, trunks of fruit trees,
crosses without names and all
are washed white. Gypsum.
Lime. Here, dirt *is* life,
shaped into utensils
and adobes—here, dirt holds
seeds soaked with irrigated
water, hoping to blossom.
Here, when canal water drains
hungry children dig in bottom
sand for crawfish. Dust storms
live in teeth, dreams and eyes.
Loose cotton blows over
empty fields months after harvest
and the roosters crow all day.
Every moment is torment
and sunrise.

My mother's home
was a bowl made of clay.
I will perish into finding
all the pieces.

INSIDE HER

Inside the woody shell of a peach pit is a nut that looks like an almond. I tried one straight from its smooth chamber, thinking it would taste like almond. It was unbearably bitter with the faintest rush of nectar.

Mother lines the peach seeds on the windowsill so they can ripen in the sun. And after a few days she eats Crimson Lady kernels, July Flames, Sweet Scarlets.

She will plant her almond roots at the edge of the lawn, nearest to the street.

Long ago, we were clingstones in her summer arms. In winters, we became scarce, white-fleshed Glaciers, Snow Fires, deciduous marionetas in fur coats, cyanide on our fermenting breath. We disregarded her chill hours that would have birthed us, rose-flushed, into spring.

Each March she blossoms white-pink flowers, blush antennae in middles. Green mesocarps release endocarps into her beaded pouch. She travels thousands of miles on the Chihuahua Trail, the Silk Road, the Andean terraces to Amazonian lowlands, floating on the sun's caravan, loosening her bolsa's drawstring. In villages, she stones pocked shells the way otters hammer mollusks open and delivers elemental zephyrs to voluptuous velvets.

ANAPRA, NEW MEXICO

Pink, turquoise, lavender
homes—an adobe
horno fills you with smoke
from the other world.

Dogs stretched out in sunlight.

Love, a mass of mud
bricks poked with pieces of hay—
tough enough to withstand fire, sun

and hail. A white jackrabbit
gutted by hawks. A row of purple
trompillo lines a road slapped down
in the middle of sand hills.

Sound: a freight train shaking
the mountains, winding around Cristo Rey,
crowning adobes submerged
in earth like pithouses.

Trumpets beckon roving mariachis
to find each other and form a band.
Disappear in the horn of song;
dust your nose with violin

pollen. Taste: a silver fever, a mercury
rio that's been here for centuries
feeding pecan trees and hope. Touch: the sun

darkening legs through a car window,
your jalopy a dull blue
pebble that will someday lodge itself
in the banks of an arroyo after one flash flood.

Home is a country of cactus
blooming bright, beautiful illnesses
from its lips. The trick is to find a succulent
green bed between vesicles and

quills. And smell is bumblebees,
factories and border patrol
sniffing your beacon of infrared
blossom wherever you go.

NO MORE ROOM

No more room for another birth. The herds have grown so rapidly. Babies moaning for milk. Milk making babies, feeding mouths. Snow fell last night, covering dirt. Where there is not a lamb, an elk, or a buffalo, there is a house, a church, a factory. We light a fire and huddle under wool. Defrost bread. Free peppers from jars. Our cells divide into more cells and fill up more space in the place we have designated home.

Winter begins with a soft, damp kiss. Whales travel south to warm, shallow lagunas and have their calves. Barnacles cling to skin like anonymous leeches. All summer, their rides engulfed plankton in Alaskan sunlight. Made enough milk. Calves are hungry. Have to grow fifty pounds a day to survive Arctic waters to come.

When Evening Becomes Stellar

Orchid sky seeps through
our window veiled with branches.

The day heals itself in amethyst
fever, entangled limbs.

Iridescent corona,
keep safe your ivory

light. My calf's tusks
are attached to the skull

of the sun. Ancestors
run under our bellies

like clans of mule deer
sinking into sky's velvet.

There is the constant beat
of prowlers' paws on the desert

drum, a watering hole
to find, there are pairs of teats

gorging with white. In the cover
of bosque and penstemon, a she

beast is born, unafraid:
with trembling legs.

Ars Poetica

The pain in the rooster's cry. My anguish, not his. He is pre-storm glimpsing electricity's gypsum, positioning without knives. We all want to catch light, drink water without thinking about toads. At the call of thunder, spadefeet emerge from hibernation and enter the acequia's bamboo ears. Without solstice would we fall?

I want geography—to know it like driftwood knows it. Offer new shapes for the macaw's tongue in the fashion of precipitation. "Ahh! Ahh!" he says as a school girl pushes "Polly want a cracker" like a veteran paleta vendor. "Ahh! Ahh! Ahh!" he replies until "Whazz up!" surfaces on the momentum of his pendulum.

Zoo verbs—envision turquoise feathers above forest canopies; close a cold eye and see dandelion seedheads along San Elizario's canal. And fear the stroke that controls the tongue. Dementia as mentor and magenta the cue stick. Halos break apart, splitting nuclei, neutrons bouncing behind closed eyes until the whole state glows ember. We need another's skin to suck until dawn.

Open window shades and feel the sun. To know it is to lack it and lick it. We're lucky to shower everyday like starfish pyrotechnics.

Drink, Drive, Go to jail. If only latchkey highway signs persuaded rain. The river fantasized by maquiladoras: a humble mail order bride, astral tassel around her waist, a rush of fools' trove at indigenous prices. *Drive friendly. The Texas way.* Tomato splats on *Welcome to New Mexico* merge with dusk in Santa Teresa, Anapra's sister. Anapra, Chihuahua just a tocaya and patrol Bronco away. Calling all agents! Erase a day's work of watering dust devil hedges and swim in the Rio Bravo with snowy egrets and colonia residents.

And Dear, I love you the way Budweisers love caliche arroyos, the way reptiles scale burrows and sore eye poppies make boys cry. And globemallow pinwheels, my little horned lizards, please guard this roost made of mud, as stellate hairs and amphibian bleating woo a monsoon from this toxic evening.

Where the Sun Rises

The heart is a cliff
dwelling.

The core of a saguaro.

A former
ocean.

It is Mesozoic,
Cretaceous, flying reptile.

O sandstone shelf—
inside you is limestone,
crushed coquina,

the inner bark
of fig trees, pounded
with lava rocks into paper.

You are thousands of miles
on an ancient trade

route by foot.
Blue-green

turquoise for copper
bells and live macaws.

Woolly
mammoth.

Fossil
and its fuel.

You are a grinding stone:
metate, molcajete.

Dried corn soaked in lime
water, swelling overnight.

Voluminous
distended kernel—

where the sun rises

you are hieroglyphic
and petrified.

Where the sun dies:
a clay pot, a bone utensil,
little buried shards.

Things rend.

Spots touch
a gold flower.

Steam
permeates
banana leaves.

A wild squash
grows by the side of the road.

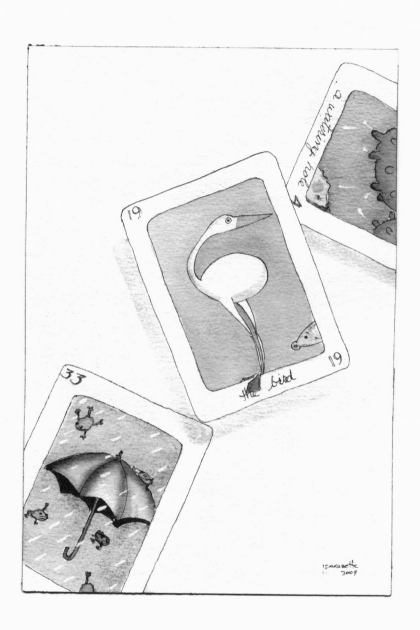

Acknowledgments

Many thanks to the editors of the following publications where many of these poems first appeared or are forthcoming: *Borderlands: Texas Poetry Review, Crab Orchard Review, Dánta: A Poetry Journal, Indiana Review, LUNA, New York Quarterly, North American Review, Prairie Schooner, Rio Grande Review, Santa Fe Broadside*, and the anthology *Places * Voices * Landscapes * Cultures* (University of Iowa Press).

Special thanks to the Atlantic Center for the Arts, the Fine Arts Work Center in Provincetown, the MacDowell Colony, the New York Foundation for the Arts, the San Francisco Foundation, and the Ucross Foundation for their support and care during the creation and preparation of this manuscript. I also wish to thank Peter, Francisco Aragón, and my traveling poetry group. Goyita and mi comadre, Ellie—my love and appreciation.

To Sandra McPherson, my immense gratitude. Thank you for providing such wisdom and generosity.